Candescent

Candescent

Poems

Linda Parsons

Iris Press
Oak Ridge, Tennessee

Cover Art: Deborah Hardison Art+Design

Book Design: Robert B. Cumming, Jr.

Iris Press
www.irisbooks.com

Library of Congress Cataloging-in-Publication Data

Names: Parsons, Linda, author.
Title: Candescent : poems / Linda Parsons.
Description: Oak Ridge, Tennessee : Iris Press, [2019]
Identifiers: LCCN 2019012508 | ISBN 9781604542578 (pbk. : alk. paper)
Classification: LCC PS3566.A77154 A6 2019 | DDC 811/.54—dc23
LC record available at https://lccn.loc.gov/2019012508

Acknowledgments

Grateful thanks to the editors of the following publications, where some of these poems first appeared:

About Place: "Confluence"
Appalachian Heritage: "Kinpeople"
Artemis: "Contrary," "Heal Soft, Not Hard"
Atlanta Review: "With Me"
Autumn Sky Poetry DAILY: "New Dog Under Gibbous Moon"
The Baltimore Review: "Divine Rods"
Blue Fifth Review: "In Tai Chi Class"
The Cape Rock: "Enough"
The Chattahoochee Review: "For Chloe, on Turning Eighteen"
Cold Mountain Review: "On Fire"
Cumberland River Review: "My Father Asks If We're Dead"
Curlew: "A Lamentation of Swans"
Cutthroat: A Journal of the Arts: "Smudge"
Delta Poetry Review: "Battered Victory," "Near Drowning"
drafthorse: "Traveling Through"
Forage: "The Voice, After All"
The Healing Muse: "Therapy Dog," "Wayfinder"
Heron Tree: "Be Peace," "Pasture"
Literary Mama: "Animal Spirits"
Louisiana Literature: "The Art of Meditation in Tennessee," "Atlantis"
The Meadow: "Forsaken," "Swept"
Mezzo Cammin: "Figs in Old October," "Humble Pie," "My Father Names Me"
Mothers Always Write: "I Love You Like a Dragon"
New Madrid: Journal of Contemporary Literature: "Grief"
New Millennium Writings: "Soft"
North American Review: "At My Father's Hospital Bedside"
One: "Fallen Idols," "No Grief," "The Secrets of Pain"

Peacock Journal: "The Home That Can't Be Lost," "The Only Way," "The Out Breath"

Pikeville Review: "Good Shepherd"

Pine Mountain Sand & Gravel: "Homing"

The Practicing Poet: Writing Beyond the Basics: "Swept" (reprint)

Psaltery & Lyre: "After Easter," "As I Meditate," "Grounding," "O Forgiveness"

Pudding Magazine: "Dogma"

Roanoke Review: "The Coming of Oranges," "Here," "Inner Work," "I Used to Be a Swan"

Silver Blade: "Rapunzel Decides"

Southern Humanities Review: "The Vale"

Still: The Journal: "Pie Lee"

Tar River Poetry: "Damascus Road"

Terrene: "Into the Water"

Writers Resist: "Stand Up"

The voice of the fire tells the truth saying, I am not the fire.
I am fountainhead. Come into me and don't mind the sparks.

—Rumi, "The Question"

You will find a fortune, though it will not be the one you seek.
But first you must travel a long and difficult road,
a road fraught with peril.
You shall see things wonderful to tell.
I cannot tell you how long this road shall be,
but fear not the obstacles in your path,
for fate has vouchsafed your reward.
Though the road may wind, yea, your heart grow weary,
still ye shall follow it,
even unto your salvation.

—Blind Seer

Buddhist Meditation Terms

Using the language and images of Buddhist meditation is another way for my writing to act as a healing practice not only for myself, but for all who hear and read it, a laying on of hands and words, of light begetting light.

Koan, a paradoxical anecdote or riddle, is used in Zen Buddhism to demonstrate the inadequacy of logical reasoning and to provoke enlightenment.

Metta is the practice of loving-kindness and openheartedness whereby practitioners direct *metta* toward themselves and others. Metta bhavana, or loving-kindness meditation, is a method of developing compassion and is a beautiful support for other awareness practices.

Samsara is life as we live it in an unawakened state, the subjective world we each create and interpret for ourselves. This world contains good and evil, joy and pain, but they are relative, not absolute, and are continually changing into their opposites. Samsara is created by our own state of mind, like the world of a dream, and it can be dissolved into nothingness just like awakening from a dream. When someone awakens to reality, to how things really are, the world is experienced in its true nature: pure, brilliant, sacred, and indestructible. There is no happiness in samsara.

—Linda Parsons

Contents

I

II

I

Part of you stays with me sprouts
through the rotten log of *good-bye*.

—William Kelley Woolfitt,
"Farm Knowledge (ii)"

Smudge

His sudden going
in winter lit one fire, now midsummer
I strike another like ancients huddled against
vast night. First, the grounding, I smudge myself,
sage bound with thread from my grandmother's
sewing box. Smoke rise, melt of burden,
bellows nearest my heart, my length, woodsy
sweet. Thresholds, where absence clanged
for days on end, dhurrie rugs, where the hackles
of odd things he left behind circled and settled
with the sheepdog. Footfalls and thumbprints,
oil musk of his pillow, irritations webbing
the eaves—leave these joists, this mortar,
far and away, far and away.

Wand of hands,
keep the scent in my head the next morning,
weave of be-all and end-all, my breath
rekindled pure and white into linen, oak
floor. When the last embers, the wild leaves,
cleansed the chairs of our living and trying,
our exhausted errors of love. Let him overturn
river rocks, skink flashing blue, heron faded
to mist. As for me, I'll root in my little Eden,
a bowl of ashes to catch the new moon,
crow feather on the sill, the remains
flapping off, mateless.

I Used to Be a Swan

Those feathered days in secret coves
when silks of ivory, wings of down
eddied through his hands. I used to be
a swan those days when pen and bill
winnowed stream for swill, my neck,
held high, lassoed the air. He laid his head
in tufted breast, no undertow till weathers
turned from spring to dire and stormed
away desire. Now hair blinds white,
gown shed at water's fold. I'll be undone
of mates, of pretty ropes and ruffled hopes,
shallows clear of seine. Needle eye on silty
hatch, black feet free of net, sun drops
low on nymphs alit, bright ease to pirouette.

Fallen Idols

On the road to Valle Crucis, I was thinking
of one anniversary rolled into another, of nothing
but pure motion and color, Grandfather Mountain
bathed in spring greens, indigos farther up,
the treeline blinding even with eyes shut.
Our tenth, but who was counting? It was time
I counted on, flashing ahead and behind,
diorama of laurel, flame azalea, time tossed
casually as a wave out the window, braking
down 194 to the crook of the Blue Ridge,
the Vale of the Cross.

We wanted to mark the day with whatever
rose rough and native from the forest floor,
like the bentwood arbors in the junkyard
outside Boone. *It'll outlast your grandbabies,*
the man said. *This here rhody and locust'll
outlast hell or high water.* I thought it might,
steeple of the gardens—twining hydrangea,
feeders, lavender mane beneath, rhododendron
ribs above, our Carolina pagoda.

It might've lasted our last winter together,
the hardest in memory. Twenty-four, but who
was counting on one storm too many—
nails popped from joints, posts gone soft,
armature listing with no rudder of goodness
and mercy? Who knew we were flying
blind in the valley of the shadow, curves
ripped with abandon, this Via Dolorosa,
this travail across hell's high waters,
in and out of time?

Good Shepherd

How he touches his nose to my leg
as I hurry with plates or dustrag, claim

without leash or license. Breathes me in,
animal to animal, heedless in the boulevards,

the brushheaps, worldly wonders of who
passed (and pissed) here before. How my day

unfolds as he rises trembly from the wicker
basket, shadows me counter to couch,

Naomi to my Ruth, whither going or staying
in the barley fields, finally the shelter of Boaz.

At the downfall of marriage, how I never
dreamed of its unquiet end, I bury my face

in his blaze of white and sable, the last man
of the house thinking me one of his flock

on the heath who calls my name *wayward*.
Eyes ghosted, nose works the air

of what dims but blooms still, keeper
from whence cometh my help.

Homing

In the day's gloaming, granddaughters raid
the honeysuckle, plunder lilies and lacecap hydrangea,
their blooming path an emergent fairy ring.
Only in the grimmest of tales would I squash
their parade on my new-mown lawn, silvery
as pebbles in Hansel's pockets. Breadcrumbs
come later, burdened with rescue in the deep-dark
wood—famine upon the land, a poor woodcutter,
a stepmother happy to strand children among beasts.

I have strewn this story like grain and the reap
of its crushing, like all omens longed for
in the dearth of childhood. I have dropped
my crusts step by step, lived until hope shone
on all that in any other forest would be lost—
the fire never dying through hungried night,
gumdrop doors eaten and eaten, no bones
but in hard telling, the moon's white bird
leading all the way back to the good father's house.

The Vale

> I am the door: by me if any man enter in, he shall
> be saved, and shall go in and out, and find pasture.
> —John 10:9

To brave the vale, to spread its curtain,
like my father on the hillock of his final pass,
our common purgatory. My father, who fingers

my knuckles with one hand, counts the abacus
of my backbone with the other. *We're in a waiting
period*, he says as if to apparitions come

for the main event, *time is winding down.*
Nothing in my own life matters, not that I share
his descent on shards of marriage vows,

that I roam the sheepfold in search of oasis.
Only that the weather is good or overcast,
lunch is coming or done. We sit skin to skin,

as never before, his hands the picture of his mother's.
Maybe she's the one in white organdy, her hair
still strawberry blond, tapping her ladies' Bulova:

Lordy, how the time goes. Maybe she's the shepherd
disguised, the one who lies down at the mouth
of thievery, both door and gatekeeper for the huddled

bleating. Let us enter the door without pleading
or birthright and be known by the one, the voice
leading us in and out to find pasture,

    fingers woven at our breasts so weary from being
    and trying, so strayed we can only be gathered.

Here

What is it about the black spring dirt
that drives him to distraction, nose planted
in earth's crotch? At fourteen, in human years
nearly a centenarian, he herds me waking
to sleeping, our pathways known beyond
breadcrumbs or moonlight. I believe the earth
itself draws him, wet with April, its rare metals,
lead and silt mysteries, inked in life's pictures—
our first joy of a certain voice to the end of all
listening. Earth that now thins his haunches
calls him from supper, my plea to *stay, stay*—
its pitch otherworldly, siren whistle he tracks
unbound, deaf to this other world,
to my clay feet dogged in earth's rank blaze
                    here, here.

The Voice, After All

Perched on my sleeve, tail flicked in my ear,
it's the voice, after all, sonorous and open,
memory bubbling up from clay. Sound cupped
like a fledgling—my first husband silver throated
on the Americana station, the soft Tennesseeisms
of my second, liquid as the river he left me for.

The voice, bubbled freshet, lifeline branched
to hapless future, hard parting, the old ache
made flesh. I'd bottle it if I could, aged oak
casks, the best of times trebled forth. I'd drink
to the gills, awash in healing, a strike to the past,
perfect cast to shallows, hearing cocked
to flurried landings, carried on water's chill breath.

Divine Rods

You must believe, and I do, believe
in the blood of my cousin thrice removed
who takes up copper rods to unearth
Civil War dead of the Franklin Campaign
whose father and grandmother witched

wells. Believe in the bartered blood
of Jesus, the Baptist cracker in my teeth.
Believe in these coat-hanger rods, plain
as the grail, as the questioning lips
at Gethsemane's table. Believe in

the fairy ring of my backyard, the already
gangly tomatoes, Kinnebecks, chard sails
hoisted, the bed of lilies sounding brief
horns on Father's Day. Believe the rods
will bend to Earth's shaky mantle

and tremble as I approach the old cistern,
plugged with river rocks, buried in green
just as the tracks where he used to park
have grassed over. And they do, the rods,
nod inward, toward whatever depth

channeled April rains for whatever
generations removed from my dailiness
under the same roof, from my turning
days' deckled pages. Believe, and I do,
in watertables untapped, tremors unfelt,

in rods divining my move from this world's
slippery source to the next, realigned
as if breath never caught or turned
askew, as if gravity's field or faith
never held me dear.

Confluence

I come late to this joining—the Clinch,
its tributary Powell, early named Pelisipi,
winding waters, by the Cherokee. Evenings

I love most, when my granddaughters
unwind, the house reflects zircons, mined
surface of river. Not my house, but my family,
years past parting—shoals, switchbacks,

snaky coves. Again at table, arms and necks
sun warmed, I give my first husband
the lion's share as his mother instructed

in my twenties. I serve and remove his plate,
refill his glass without resentment or ire,
the outlier who eddied away, the red rover
called to the other side. *Let me come over*,

I ask, the rope less taut between us—
knot by knot, he mends memory's seine.
We sift rock and silt, the epic flood's

devastation. Tonight brim and bluegill
are striking. Norris above, Melton Hill
below dam old levels against new spill,
release familiar schools I swim

    with currents easing. He sets
    a lantern at the brow of the dock.

Traveling Through

To my first husband, let me say all those years
we burned the night oil up I-81 from Knoxville
to your parents in north Jersey, you were right
about the blind of fog dropping its soft hammer
on tail lights ahead. Right about the speed I double-
dog dared, thinking I could out-blue the Shenandoahs,
make Bethlehem by dawn. Right that whatever
wreckage stalled on the yellow line would be
our Waterloo, our vanished horizon still time
away, never mind my fool's errand, the children
tucked like your mother's cannoli in sugared sleep,
precious cargo she called them, barely stirring
as we raced on apart.

To my mother, I still see you at the Greyhound
station after our visit, a guest in my house
as I was in yours, shedding each other like coats
out of season, arguments stale as that depot
on Magnolia, seats torn, half-smoked smokes,
Coke gumming the floor. Let me say the kids
needed dinner before the Music City bus boarded,
so I left you then as I wouldn't now, with those people,
no car or extra dollar to their name, left with a pat
on the hand, cheek turned as brakes hissed
their going, neither waving *goodbye, goodbye,*
running along the silver length for a last glance,
blowing what kisses we had left.

To my father, owning the highway's mirage
of heat and speed, let me say I was the one
waiting till you circled home, sales soared
on a smile and a shoeshine. The one unversed
in fourth and goal, second down, play by play
you armchair quarterbacked, home from your swath
of territory. Let me say I'm the one with the tray
of greens and pintos in assisted living where you
wonder if enough players are on the field
and how did I find you in the dead of winter,
the road snowed over, though outside May
blooms her heart out. Let me say I will always
find you, alone on the bench, hypnotized
by the whiteout, the crowd a roar in your head.
Just as you found me, uncompassed,
without a ride to childhood's remains,
veering into the constellated dark.

To my daughters, let me say I sowed no wild
oats before nineteen, quoting Ruth at the altar:
Whither thou goest, and so on, sour even then
in my ear and mouth. I had not spit black seeds
across the kitchen I swept and polished to keep
the ship yar, my mother in dress whites commanding
the stern. To say I flew off willy-nilly you know
too well, your pillar of childhood dissolved to salt,
my leaden baggage nothing like precious cargo.
Let me say there's time to raise my flag with yours,
our shifting winds none could foresee or batten
down, time to raise our wild *whither we goest*,
spit change across the black sea.

To my second husband, let me say the books,
some yours, some mine, are still talking in their rows,
unlike us, after your leaving, I might say, like a thief
in the night. The gazebo you trucked in for my fiftieth
is just as violet in the gloaming, the porch just as pleasant,
haint blue the bane of ill will, wicker an embrace.
Most of our years, let me say, were an anchor against
the hard past, our best words' fertile field, lying
now in rust and stubble of daily disappointments.
In wormy forbearance the gardens fruit ever on,
fed on your absence. To say fear begat our prophecy
is to blame the Earth for its turning, which I sit
and watch unfailingly, saying to moon and sun
lit with the same old glory, *Tell me that one again.*

To my granddaughters, let me say life is a coin,
the rarest Indian head, dullest copper, the backwoods
you sneak to behind the creek, the tracks your mother
tells you *never, never*, rails trembling with transit
where you balance the coin, your ears to the ground's
thunder. Notice how honeysuckle chokes the fence,
the wild rose—then step back and wait, *please step
back* as the iron horse barrels past. And though
you know to cool it before touching, you will anyway,
before it's ready. Let me imagine your two heads
together in wonder at the power that blew your hair,
shut your eyes, the metal flattened into something
indiscernible, something changed in an instant,
the future white hot in your hands.

My Father Asks If We're Dead

Perhaps because of
her turquoise eyes, voice the sweet echo
of her mother's, my sister pries open
our tightlipped father easier than I.
Their visits at assisted living end in tears.
He calls her, pleading: *Where am I?*
Am I dead? Are you? His loneliness waits
in a busy station of bad florescence,
tobacco stains, workaday faces flashing past
to adventure, the bus or train he flags down
slowed to its last stop.

We steady his steps
but cannot join him in the departure line,
ours the rush of faces to elsewhere as he calls
Hello, hello, is there anyone left? We cannot
return him to the arched porch of his grandparents'
house on N. Second in east Nashville or the bungalow
off Shaw AFB where he yelled through five-card
stud in the throes of Hurricane Hazel. We cannot
nail his papery memory like a lunch menu
to the wall, repeating peas, repeating okra.
We cannot even know whether we live or die
in this warp of time and blank sorrow,
whether to sing out loud or pinch ourselves
when we walk from his darkened room
into bright midday, half-blind,
half-crazed for life.

Kinpeople

Like all men bleeding out
on the battlefield, he wants his mother.
He wants Sunday dinner, the farm-fresh girl
creamy and veined as bluejohn, the calves'
brains she scrambled with eggs of a morning.

In his fog of confusion,
my father wants her shyness, coming
home to simpler times before the war,
the strawberry blond who covered
her mouth when she laughed.

Some days I tell him
she's frying those apples he loves, others
I say she's thirty years gone. He searches
among the casualties, the unexploded
shells, limbs cockeyed as ragdolls
on the beachhead.

He leans in closer:
Are you my kinpeople? Yes, I am, I say.
I'm your kinpeople. He searches on
for flares of the once known, for Annie Louise
pouring tea in the Fostoria, not slicing
the roast till he sits. He picks through
bloodied rocks for shards of her name.

The Only Way

<blockquote>
There are a hundred ways to kneel and kiss the ground.
—Rumi
</blockquote>

Honor your grief, every whim and chore,
in the checkout lane, the kalamatas he used to buy

too rich for your blood, in the used book shelves,
rank pages he nosed like a dog searching

for its president. However you've grieved
in the past is but an anthill to this wail and rent,

a whisker, paltry dust of gone years. Though
grief may deceive in brocade and silks, it thieves

into that rag and bone shop you call *heart*,
unravels every thread down to hard gristle.

Honor your grief with ragged breath and privation
in the body's dark cell despite how the blithe

world cries *enough*. Wait not so patiently
for the Full Flower Moon to shower its blessings,

Mars in red opposition. Turn in place, feather
your bare nest, until the only way is to kiss

the ground with pocked knees, grabble roots
like a flathead cat screwed into mud until finally

sun wrests the scales from your eyes.

New Dog Under Gibbous Moon

I see the moon and the moon sees me,
God bless the moon and God bless me.
—Children's lullaby

Though it waxes gibbous above the gazebo,
more than half full but not fully illuminated,
we bark at night's starry door—me, for the moon
in its heaven to shower mercy and purpose;
the new dog, for me to notice only him in my turning
to others hung there, water bearer and hunter,
our constellated brothers. For I am his one light,
milk-faced, reflective. His ewe to be corralled
in the hills, these days more wayward than not.

In the longer orbit from crescent to sphere,
a child's song rises: *God bless the one
that I can't see.* The night sky sorrows over
that one, mate gone from my yard, my life,
why I wail to the ether, glowing bodies
deaf with degrees of change, realignments,
waxing only to wane. Geometry has its way
with us. The sheepdog and I seek goodness
in the eclipsed dark, even faithful Sirius,
Canis Major, at his master's heel, the bull
still light-years away.

The First Night Pain Doesn't Wake Me

I awaken surprised to have slept without
the nightlong ache in my hip, moan
slipping out at two or three, sciatica or radiated
back strain, with every step and turn
until the lack is like morning itself, newborn.
Not much touched it—ice, yoga's cat and child,
tai chi's white stork, Celtic body prayer
in supplication—until I scraped my bowl
empty of longing, until I sat in the dust
busking my tarnished tune and bowed
in gratitude for ache, for moan, for loss
at the hot marrow, believing in their forever on,
until I invited the hours to the side porch
for oranges and ginger tea, no longer
            friendless and warring.

II

The precious pot containing my riches
becomes my teacher in the very moment it breaks.

—Milarepa

Rapunzel Decides

At marriage knell,
my hair thickens and I no more scissor
at the mirror, my barber grandfather
shadowed in bas-relief. I no more
chop and snip nearly to the bone,
going by pure feel. My hair

honeysuckles
the fencepost, too much wah-wah
to notice how it twines and silvers.
My hair fabled and regaled, retold
by firelight, braided by tribal mothers
until it grows in largesse, encircles

wolves and black swans,
a blood moon. In the village square,
rung wide and far, great awakening
at the embattled gate: no more waiting
for the prince to ascend the fool's ladder,
no more fairytale end. My hair

the enchantress,
her forbidden rampion, skein of silk
more precious than birdsong, all I own
high in the tower, my warbling onliness
loose in the straw winds over river
and creek that calls nightly
in plea and release:

Let it down,
let it down.

Grounding

Root yourselves, the teacher says, sink into the subflooring,
be one with the fibers of pine, scuffed boards, your feet
unmovable as granite embedded through eons. I come
to tai chi as root, rock, wind, cloud. Sometimes I bend
to gather bundles of grain, sometimes to spread white stork's
wings or strike my enemy the tiger. I come because I have
lost my way in the streets of town, because my ground
was stolen by one I thought would never uproot house and home,
because now, in synchronous rows on Sunday afternoons,
I see nothing can stand beneath my feet but the solemn
and lovely earth, the molten fire within it, cirrus rags above.
No one can steal my ground while I pivot pigeon toed, hips
square to the green wall, unmoved in knowing what is lost
is yet seen, the beak of my hand set to preen my iridescence.

The Home That Can't Be Lost,
the Gold That Never Stops Shining

       The breath, like the heart,
knows its home: amber light at the lintel,
haint-blue porch, door bleached by high summer.
The breath knows even when I've forgotten—
my grandmother's house on Russell, rooms
dreamed into being, my own veined walls
caulked and spackled. I've waited years
to be met on these steps, to be the fall rose
in its last rouge, the topmost figs slick
with sweet despite the near cold, a prodigal
unsure of feast or table. I've prayed
for blessed time to rebraid my scars,
sitting cross-legged in early dark, when
the breath could've told me to plant
in the unknowing—the mind a pond,
a meadow, the cosmos pebbled in dust,
a lotus wholly at home in the muck—no longer
roaming dogpaths or wilderness, no longer
             a motherless child knocking.

Heal Soft, Not Hard

for Rita Quillen

Unhammer your chest
into June afternoons where gloaming
never ends, march of cedars in the feathered
dying west. Though wounds gap deep as culverts,
ditch lilies planted while you slept trumpet
the evermore. On heart pine floor, in sorrow's
bleat and moan, the afterbirth weighs labors
lost. A bath is drawn by unseen hands, citrus
and geranium dabbed at your wrist like milk
warmed for Wednesday's child so full of woe,
Thursday's child so far to go. Heal soft,
not hard, knead steel to flesh and flesh
to gloss. Go where you will, your native soil
to bale with sweat and wheat and swale
        till last light summons first.

On Fire

> We live in a perpetually burning building,
> and what we must save from it, all the time, is love.
> —Tennessee Williams

Embers in the gloaming spit like tickseed
from grasses, like sparks freed from molten layers

below—tiny fires too multiplied for the jars
and reach of granddaughters. Even purple light

draping high-hatted oaks cannot dull the goldmound
spirea, the spider lilies' lumen, nor quiet the youth

of the new sheepdog at my feet. If our shaky earth
is indeed a timber house perpetually afire, where

only love can rush in and save us, let its burning
cover the ground we live and perish on, maddened

with loss in between. Let it flare and singe
our eyebrows, the nests of squirrels and mockers,

release their chittering at our malice aforethought.
Sepia photos of great-greats we stack by the curb,

the recipe box with handwritten cards, our back
and forth still maddened with heartache, uneasy

purification. We rest a moment to clear our lungs,
take the tally of disaster versus rescue. We count

our blessings, though the blackened corners
            flake off at our touch.

Damascus Road

My neighbor writes to say she wouldn't be
writing if it weren't a matter of life and death,

if my burning bushes along the road weren't
blocking her view and she hadn't nearly

been T-boned three times. So I'm thinking of
Judy Blue Eyes seeing life from both sides now,

never thinking to look from my neighbor's view.
I'd let the bushes go for privacy, my last year

swaddled in grief and remorse, walking
my alone road, every burning step a pitfall.

As Saul, zealous Pharisee and persecutor,
became Paul the follower, blinded in a flash

of vision, who am I but my own weary
traveler transformed, blasted new into traffic

without looking both ways? What road
is this but the street called Straight,

longest in Damascus, where at the end
in a home of food and fire, the laying on

of hands restores sight and bearing,
where again I am filled and scales

        drop from converted eyes?

Grief

You know the sound before it reaches the curb,
exhausted air brakes, quarrel of tokens rubbed

faceless—you turn from whatever gives shape
and meaning to your day—the aisle of cantaloupes,

ripe or green, the page you've read twice. You turn
because the horn blasts your name, your forwarding

address, and the door swings open. Women lift made-up
eyes as you find your seat, sway as gears downshift.

Whatever route you have chosen might be the dream
of the House of Mirrors, fogged and elusive. *Let me off,*

you say to the whistle of wind, the shattered windows,
it's my stop! Even the childhood montage of Chesterfield

ads and Brylcreem barbwires your heart, though surely
up ahead is Woodland or Porter Road, your grandmother's

call on trips to Harvey's downtown, at the entrance
the mynah birds' caged caw. *I've done my time,*

you're crying now to anyone who will listen—
passersby, street dogs, the man with wheels for legs

selling pencils on Broadway, the driver who keeps
driving because where else does he have to go?

Enough

Enough of the dying dog between us,
his boniness through fur like seed pearls,

muzzle I've stroked thinking each time
the last. We wait for the needle pulled

from the satchel. I spoon the floor to cradle
his head, you've returned to a house divided,

our small talk barely keeping the walls
upright, the closet bereft of your clothes.

Enough that this old dog watched over
our remains, the rooms, my baskets and books,

an utterance by my side. Enough of our
blithe inattention, our redemption impossible

on the flowered rug, his bag of bones
flown or sunken wherever the spirit lights—

even that of a dog is holy, my crook
and shepherd unto the psalmed hills.

Enough of time borrowed, it was only
borrowed here on the parched earth

neither whole nor rent to our liking, love
splayed like his ruff in the wind, the last

place we've come to, followed and scented
even so, this dead weight of dog between us.

A Lamentation of Swans

Oh, what will I do, what will I say,
when those / white wings / touch the shore?
—Mary Oliver

Unbow solemn heads, sister swans,
though only birchbark, amber, Belleek
on windowsill, dropleaf, bookshelf.
Rise on swift currents, reed basket
in the rushes, our Miriam no one
but ourselves astonished by our lightness,
wingspread up and over
what weather has wrought.

Hawk bears his vision quest, crow
cocks a wizened eye, owl drops
her prize of tiny bones. Lament not
loss or error. A kinder hearth feathers
near, mercy rains where nimbus broods.
It starts in blue holes unaware,
ponds unstirred by wind,
that smallish cove within.

Phantom

Strange the great presence in absence—
book I remembered on the second shelf
of the red bookcase, next to Flannery

and Ole Fred, rounding the corner to bare
wall, or brushing my left hand, indentation
on the ring finger from years of gold.

The mind plays tricks, clasps the gilt frame
of imagined life even after the moving truck
with his furniture barrels off, even after

I sit shiva with my grief, days unraveled
partly by my own device, and I have, thread
by knotty thread, woven a new silken skin.

Ghost pain, phantom pain, a limb lopped
clean, the dead bee's sting. We are good
amputees, efficient little starfish and lizards,

regenerating feet and tails in the shadows
where no one watches us spin and weep,
where no one sees me turn a corner

in the dark before bed, giving wide berth,
my body's radar still beeping and flashing
to sidestep a bookcase no longer there.

The Secrets of Pain

The Secrets of Pain, I read the sign and smile,
knowing it's *pan* in the patisserie of brioche
and baguettes sold on the boulevard in Valence
d'Agen, each layer papered as Maundy ash,
airy as the cottonwood seeds whispering past,
a world from my floured counter in Tennessee.
I read and smile, knowing the secret ingredients:

butter from the Charolais near Auvillar,
oven salvaged from a country *grandmere*,
a flick of the wrist bringing bloom after bloom
to rise over earthenware rim. What more
does it take to fill belly or table, even hearts
unsated year after year, scorched at the edges,
hardened by salt and long stirring? What more
can be sliced from the tough middle, grown cold
in refusal to travel the unleavened divide?

Soft

I am soft as the fatted calf the prodigal
comes home to. Soft as the corona of fat

ringing the pâté Christophe served in my rose-
hung gîte. Soft with *le canard*, scored, seared

in honey, balsamic, shallots. My thighs soft
with Roquefort, marbled in all the tender places,

languished in Deep France without squats
on waking to work. Soft as cobbles

along the Way of St. James, pilgrims winding
narrows to Santiago de Compostela. Soft

as millet wheeled to Sunday market, Auvillar's
baskets of coquilles, macarons, fleur de sel.

Centuries soft in alcoves, the must of L'église
Saint-Pierre, porcelain tributes to beloveds,

my reach through time's gray veil. My knees
soft in daily descent past the old convent

to write nothing soft, nothing limping,
to strop lines, hammer to a sheen. Light falls

on my knapsack, soft as the callas in high
May. This camino a weightless field of stars

at the confluence of country and river.
The Garonne braids the Tennessee,

a ribbon lacing Pyrenees to Appalachians,
uphill and down, this daughter wandered far.

For Chloe, on Turning Eighteen

Write a letter, I've heard it said, a letter
to yourself at eighteen, though you may be
forty or sixty, as far from eighteen as nobody's
business. It's your business to look back
at any age you choose if it's done with class
and grace and not crying too much in your beer.
There may be some crying, in fact, some longing
and sorrow, the usual human predicament
brought on in November when maples slough
their riding hoods and it aches just watching
them melt into the good earth. Turn away
from the past before your feet begin to harden
to salt. No hardening allowed in this letter,
no regret at what might have been
because all the paths taken were yours alone.

Your quiet doe eyes and even doe breath
drew them to you surely as the hunter's moon
washed the pebbles that saved you
from the gingersnap door, gumdrop chimney,
curl of unmentionable smoke. Or, if you must,
pack the past lightly in your rucksack, no wool
socks, no toothbrush, just the essentials—
Cinnamon's chestnut flanks, your grandparents'
land a branched lifeline, a mirror you carry
in your hip pocket and sometimes hold
to the sun, setting small fires of memory.
Sign it now, the letter, sign with flair,
and not a little blood, in witness of
your becoming, of the baskets and years
you filled with chicory and gloriosa,
tossing back your thick doe hair.

The Coming of Oranges

Nothing about it is pretty, habit carried
from my grandmother, timid woman
behind Coke-bottle glasses cutting oranges

for Christmas in a compote dish, sugared
in her country way, shredded coconut,
apples. Nothing easy about the dull knife

he once sharpened on the whetstone, old
habits forsaken. And nothing but navels
will do, rind pried bit by bit, coating

my thumbs with pith, the essence of citrus
in winter's grip. I should take it as a sign
in the East, these fists spitting juice

on the counter, swaddled against the inner
sweet, a sign the year has wrought, hard
pressed and tearing flesh, when all I wanted

was a bowl of unriven suns. When all
I asked was love's labor gained, light's
advent pouring into humble quarters,

the still point of waiting for hopes to align.
There's nothing pretty in the silenced night
except, as wise men over dreams of sleep

keep watch while others turn from banked
fires, orange flame borne high and long
to pierce the darkest deep.

In Tai Chi Class

> Remember me as one who woke up.
> —The Buddha

I carry:
the tiger who crushes the basket of my heart
my eyes rubbing salt from the wound
bird's tail grasped and missed
my hips square to the green wall
silk threading my bamboo trunk
my shattered wings like lotus lanterns
silence approaching the bearded mountain
my torn chi as the white stork
bouquet of my chest, now wilted, now open
my missteps at the mirror
my hands like clouds

> *Appear to close the ancient entrance,*
> *for the night, oh the night is coming.*

I remember:
how we crossed purposes, regret/no regret
our separate homes, red maples touching
the pearls we caught though deaf and blind
time given in first hope, ending in second hope
our sorrow passed in frail teacups
all we lost and found, willows yielding
all we are and are not, willows unyielding
none is blameless, none is burdened
beyond bearing

> *Strike the tiger as she naps on the mudbank.*
> *Will she wake in Full Thunder Moon? Will I?*

Swept

My hands grip handle, pendulum
swing on Grandmama's steps, broom
falls apart at the seams. I the broom,
the unsewn seam. Her dime gripped,
this good job of work swept through

time, spending the peace between
women and men. I the steps Granddaddy
trips, belly beerful, his way undone.
I the storm's eye, this good work,
this right on time, for buffalo nickel

or dime. Sweep it gone, this dust
of a girl who spins on the head of a pin.
I the rust, the splinter, swept under carpet
or rug, bone in my arm unable to rest.
I the dirt hidden and piled, song

for my supper, this house of uneasy
belong. I the woman disturbing the peace,
my handle gripped, I the web
husband leaves in the eaves, spidering
book and shelf. I the broomstraw

stuck in his craw, cain raised in cloud
of days. I the pendulum sweeping him
gone, coin of the realm outspends
our fine design. I the hands, the railing
tripped, I the seam unknowing the rip.

I the steps leapt two at a time, we
the bellyful having enough. I the eye
gathering storms, the peace swept here
alone. I the haze, tune unhummed,
that good clean sweep the long way home.

O Forgiveness

It creeps up from behind, a trick pulling
the wool, someone who says *close your eyes*,
taps your crown, trails fingertips down

the side of your head. You'd swear an egg
cracked ever so gently, the white seepage,
yolk rivered to your ears. Or how my grandmother

sat me on a stool, stood behind to plait my hair,
my muscles gone rubbery, her touch light
as a foot on the Kenmore treadle. Truth be told,

it's more an onrush, the Lower Ninth Ward
overwhelmed though the Army Corps
of Engineers vouched no levee would breach,

sweeping to sea my resolve to clasp our years'
turned locket till death do us part. It comes
ripping off the blindfold that strands me

on the ledge, a pyramid of Flying Wallendas
on my thin shoulders. It comes unshuttering
the windows, uprooting the maple I always

knew would hit the house. It comes when it
comes, on no one's timetable, whether the creek
does or don't rise, whether I split the ground

of his leaving finding nary a drop to drink,
whether my heart still bleeds from the corner
or has staunched the flow with alum. Whether

    I'm ready or not, *olly-olly-in-free*,
    a new day lifts its gaze from the dust
    of summer drought.

Therapy Dog

Leafed out like a bloodgood maple
in my meditation chair, my focus
ungainly over flagstone and sedum,

downpour of emotion. Feet flat
to the cold, I am alone with intention.
The mindful bell conditions his coming,

as others are called in the wake
of smoldering disaster, when buildings
quake and crumble, papery hands

grasp the long forgotten, when
a child wounded in unspeakable places
cannot say where or how. Come

herders and retrievers, velveteen
with hot breath, to unjangle nerves
in courtrooms, sniff out grand mal

and stealth of dying, when the smoke
and wail clear, and those left living
lift their dark glasses for the first time

since falling so far so fast, stash
their canes in the closet. In the daily
mantra of metta, come snowy blaze

to soften wrongs, lay back ears
for a sweet lick of spoon. Come
shawl my ankles, wet nose to knee,

both taproot and compass
for my straying. No matter whence
no matter where, *Come.*

The Art of Meditation in Tennessee

Ah invites the Divine, *om* gives thanks
to the Divine. The breath wheels me
to summer, creek back of the field, icy
at my ankles. *Ah* and *om*, relax the fist
of my heart, loss pushed from my belly,
a rowboat from shore. Rest in its rocking
to and fro, breathe in peace, breathe out joy.
Heat bugs deafen the understory, blacksnake
twines in honeysuckle, crawdad pinches
till it thunders, leeches suckle shin, river
mourns and bleeds. Return to the rowboat,
the change it portends, one life astern,
one rides the bow, neither here nor there.
My household eddies down—dropleaf table,
cherry secretary—it was never mine to keep.
Bless this threshold with burning sage,
invite the Divine, *om* and *ah*. Rooms
breathe in peace, breathe out joy. Give
thanks for ringing footsteps, spit shine
his shoes, charcoal and ecru, emergence
within exit. The breath, when nothing else
remains, how it rinses clean the wild
freshets. In the end, all is left, all Divine.
Breathe in peace, breathe out joy.

III

The other side of the world, they say, is a door
where I'll find my life again.

—Charles Wright, "Littlefoot, 34"

The Buddha Gives His Fire Sermon
at the Retreat Center in Tazewell, Tennessee

Burning, we're all burning.
Until we cease grasping for more,
for what is not, until we stop wanting
the field flower to be a rose—we and all
beyond us burn—the rods in our flawed
eyes, the perfect sky, molecules
in the lemon-ginger water, clank
of pots, endless turning in strange beds
this country-dark night that thrums
like neurons in the brain.

I warm hands over embers sparked
in the high meadow, release cares
like long-boned sycamores flanking
the Powell River. Surely the heat
of meeting and joining here will melt
latches weathered to rust, spill the silo's
golden dust, tamp away misdirection.
Yet everything burns. I cling to the skin
I know best. Blood singes crown to foot,
flint on flint, all friction and candescence,
all filaments and charge.

My roommate knits in low light,
her movements shadow puppets on the wall.
The clicking atoms do what they do.
The bell sings. Silence calls, cool
and clear. I remove my shoes, my blame.
I slip from the body I thought I knew.
I step out on the summer porch. A breeze,
a fullness of stars. A friend may stop by,
someone not seen in a good while,
but I have no expectations. I wait,
open as prayer cast on brown currents.

Two Dragons

> If you are irritated by every rub,
> how will your mirror be polished?
> —Rumi

Oil and water, says the psychic,
touching my temples, neck, shoulders.

Spectra from his fingertips channel
long silence from my throat chakra,

swallowed voice I recognize only
as distant family in the refrain of worn

marriage in a house of dragons—
water dragon, fiery yet bendable, metal

dragon, alloy of resolute flame and steel.
The room flashes violet and gold, my throat

opens like time's ravine leapt across,
bucket sloshing, in honeymoon years

half-full, near the end seeping wordless.
Use citrus oil, the psychic says, to clear

the chakra, speak daily or lose your footing
on the rocks. Release the body's lyric

from its perch, strike fire on and off
the page. Speak the aura of oil's rainbow,

or nothing of sweetness will stand,
your life flown to cinders and ash.

Humble Pie

Flaky, that crust, so lean and light,
oh the taste of humble pie. Not cherry,
not berry, not peach or lime, but pride
stripped down to humbleness. That man,
my twin, shoes by the door, fed me a piece
of that humble pie. Piled deep and high,
I mixed it right, added salt, half his, half mine,
no harm, no fault. Flour the counter, roll out
plans, the universe laughs at leaving men.
Nothing lasts forever, the Buddhists say,
nothing lasts long. All God's children
don't get along. Suffering happens, woe
be us, put hands together, pray to the sky,
suffer that butter in humble pie. Pie, pie,
that humble pie.

Make a space in one small room, strike
a flame to fill the gloom, sit with sorrow,
sit and chill, there you'll weep on heartbreak
hill. A new day mends that awful tear,
turns bitter to sweet, turns truth to dare.
Heal soft, not hard, when it's said and done,
new cinnamon me upon the tongue.
Me, me, me oh my, better than any humble
pie. Stir it in, good and hot, never forget
that humility pot. Keep it near, near
as fire that scalds your mouth and burns
your ear. Heap old fears in the soul's
dark night, remember that work, so dear
and wise, remember to remember
that humble pie.

Atlantis

When I'm still in my coat the winter night
you drove away, not a deer in the headlights
but hit square on, it's the lost history that deepens
the wound. Alphabet of twenty-four years
translatable by only we two—what book, film,
person, where or when, you remember, the one
we loved or couldn't abide. Almanac of kindred
journeys: the talk simpatico, Yellowstone's unearthly
thermal pools, the Badlands, horsehair bracelet
from Cody I wear most days. Time imprinted
like letterpress, rolling in reams.

If men disdain the look back, that salty pillar,
I say memory is a glass-bottomed boat skimming
murkiness below, an undersea city of spires and turrets,
winnowed grain, pomegranates at market, people staying,
after all, to weather their storms. I say the foundation
holds through ruination—distrust, retreat to walls
ever higher, vain errors of our ways. A great city
of our making and unmaking beneath dailiness
apart, in our death a little life in and of memory,
like those silvery shrubs dotting the prairie,
its leaf, when we rubbed it, you remember,
bloomed of sage.

Forsaken

Here the chestnut rails from his uncle's place
he said would last a hundred years, arbor

arched for the path, wedding bower to please
me early on. Fine Crab Orchard stone,

quarried on the Plateau. Sweet their joining—
wood muscled gray above, iron swirled

pink below. Until weather came down
on our miscalculations, rails fallen

to disrepute, thrown behind the shed, until
rain and grubs hungered to the mealy heart.

My first winter alone, these rotten fiddlesticks
I lug to the road, raise like cabers over my head

and toss ringing, Scots blood thicker than I knew.
Someone with a taste for fire will stop in the night,

take their measure, their former selves, and ours,
once a reverberation, plank on plank as hammers

sang the livelong day, full voiced, without sweat,
ache, or tiring. Unforsaken in the oneness of May.

Pasture

When thoughts arise on well-worn paths,
let passing breath bend fountain grass,

stretch out near gate's hinged swing.
Your way, good or dire, choose where

attention lands: goldfinch stitch on
locust fence, Three Sisters' stubble field—

or merely mirrored pond. The senses graze,
rain or shine, this pasture of the mind.

Your give or take of peace dropped slow,
this room of heart's require, uncloud

your thoughts, unending storm, your
troubled yesteryear. Let dead be dead—

be upturned stone, be foxfire glow,
earth melting latent snow. When thoughts

arise, sing high the body's tune. Return,
return, to cress beneath your feet,

return to real and true.

After Easter

The airy headroom, where the egg flattens,
that's where you begin. A tug as the frail

shelter gives, pastel dyes the map of thumb
and forefinger. Beginning is the hardest, not

piercing the white mantle, though a lip clings
to the shell, bloom of outermost coating,

and ruins the perfect oval. So many ruins—
the long night limping uneven roads to Samaria,

the morning after, even as the stone rolls
away in wonder and exclamation, our eyes

shielded to day's cold light. The membrane
next, shed like stepping out of a slip, like so much

we slip past and into, never meaning pain
or death, practicing compassion on our floor

cushion or under the Bodhi tree. It comes
down to the rich middle you always believed

was present, brilliant eye in the eggy cup,
the center yoked somehow to faith

in and of mercy, that magnificent yellow,
true color of forgiveness, that small peep

of joy rising whether you deserve it or not.

Battered Victory

Winged victory, classic and Grecian,
I tell the sculptor, whose Vicksburg drawl

drapes my unclothed shoulders, whose hands
are already sizing me up, already imagining

the muscle of clay, ochre or steel gray dug
from the Carolina Piedmont, not so foreign

from my own karst and foothills west of Asheville,
my body more ebb and flow than terrain,

more Bosc pear than vessel, one breast
cupped for heft, for measure, where light

strikes where, crescent of hipbone, his finger
along my Caesarian scar, forty years healed,

too sensitive and shy for lovers—but there,
at the *mons pubis,* a shiver, like intimacy, passes

creator to model in the studio of white dust
that rides the soles of my shoes, that after firing

to bisque and glaze, will grace mantle or tabletop,
wings burnished teal or rust, another clash

    with my hard night's better angels,
    another battered victory.

My Father Names Me

My father rushes in, late as usual,
my name fresh on his lips, not my mother's
choice, she told me later, still waking,

groggy from chloroform, birth certificate
blank on the sheets. As usual he was late,
her choice already made, not *Linda*,

another name engraved on the locket.
His choice, she told me later, the song
on the radio as he drove to the hospital:

We pass on the street, my heart skips
a beat, I say to myself, Hello, Linda.

Still green and waking to a child
in their midst—her pencil-thin skirt,
his white bucks—a choice they made

to mend fraying ends, my name meaning
beautiful. A foreign world on their lips,
too vast and impossible to shake them

awake, something beautiful frayed
even then, a family unending soon upended,
chloroformed song on my rosebud lips,

a name like and unlike any other.
Their choice already engraved,
my father rushes in, late as usual.

Contrary

Blessed are the contrary, accent on the second syllable in mid-South talk—as my sainted grandmother let fly when I ragged on about Polly's market, bartered dime to quarter for candy cigarettes. Contrary at the edge of my mother's serration, my sass not to dispute her word. Contrary like a pressure cooker's spew of soupbeans on the wallpaper after years of lightly, lightly on eggshells. Not *have a blessed day*, but blessed be contrariness for the sake of my brain and mouth and voice that won't be shushed, even by my ownself. My ownself that rents sackcloth at the mirror of *mea culpas* for things this mouth upended. Contrary, not meaning meanness or gossip or mock, but a by God honest tongue. Woe to them that can't meet on the dotted line, toe to toe, can't pick that bone to the blood heart, where the rubber meets the real. Call it age or a confluence of contrariness, rivered down the ancestral stream. Above all, let me be kind, let me deliver the biscuits and butter of kindness in a wicker basket clothed in linen to the least of us, love as its double cousin—no cheek to turn, stone to unturn, no backtalk to walk back—just a table polished with Pledge, just as I am with only one plea: to be and be heard, all of me neither sour nor sweet, then to lean in close, and lean closer, to listen.

I Love You Like a Dragon

for my granddaughters

I love you like a dragon in spiky spininess
that wallops barns to tinder, thunders woodland

floor. In scary thorns pricking girly curls
and nightly cricket trail. In mountain's toes

that scoop earth's foes, scales raging blustery
skies slice down to burning questions—chocolate

or apple pie? In hot breath, crafty yellow eye,
I set the meatiest afire. I love you bold and bolder,

I seek the sweeter hearts. Unafraid of the darker
deep, door creaked in dream-tossed sleep,

my pointy wings wing high, wing low, sisters
sheltered here beneath. What do I love, my darlings,

what do I love most of all? A grounded love
so sure of flight, without manners, without

slight. The brightest love, through time
and place, the fiercest love no one dare fight.

A toothless love that has no bite,
unbound and bounding, sear delight.

Stand Up

> Sit down, sit down, sit down, sit down,
> sit down, you're rockin' the boat.
> —Frank Loesser, *Guys and Dolls*

Lo these many years,
I the peacemaker, the walker on eggshells,
the biter of lips, the please pleaser, the clay
not the molder, the stream not the bank,
the moss not the rock, the stern not the bow,
queen of if only I'd said, if only I'd done.
Lo I say unto you, I'm done with sit down,
sit down, done with the broom and its dust,
old love and its rust, the future walking right
out the door. Hear me, I'm here with a voice
from the gloom, the moon-filled room, rise
of wing to beat the band, however long
I must stand is how long I'll rock,
rock, rock the boat.

Grab this, strike this,
be peace in the deafest of ears, be this,
if you can bear the whole of me holding
up half the sky's the limit, be aware,
O beware the end is near, the end of silence
of reticence of swallowing it down, choking
on what can't be told in mixed company.
I'll be clearing my throat, unbending
my knee, strapping my heart to my sleeve.
The one speaking aloud who sings without
pause, the unturned cheek, the unshut eye,
who digs her heels in this wide-awake
moment and lets the mother tongue fly.

Oracle

He's still here, says the clairvoyant,
revealing the tarot, card by card. Here,
though I've smudged the house with wands
of sage, rid the walls of broadsides,
sold and gifted books. Here, though I sit
on a buckwheat cushion in early dark,
shuffling my deck of metta, the Major Arcana
spread before me. I tap one of three stacks,
offer loving-kindness: *May we be free of fear,
may peace be with us*, the leaving and the left,
our shared trespass. Karma is strong in the cards,
she says, and will hit like a locomotive,
tip the scales of my ascendant Libra toward
something just, something right coming round.
Though nothing is fair in this dream of life,

our waking akin to a dream, said the Buddha,
acceptance of what is, our only magick wand.
One morning, the clairvoyant tells me,
I will wake starved for light—and paint over
the old, crack open the wall between dining
and living rooms. One day the Emperor
will appear, redhaired, tall, steadfast, and we
will be easy as children. He will speak in tongues
of blueprints, weight bearing, distribution
of light, an engineer. I wait for the redheaded
stranger. For the cold knife of deliverance,
the future's caesarian birth. Wait for the train
to jump its tracks, for the light's jubilation.
I wait for my walls to come down.

As I Meditate

      the riverrock of consciousness
slick with moss and missteps, sways side
to side from the first plop, scarce light
at surface, cove darkened with samsara.
Depths greeny then sallow, my world-
worn weight follows it down. The koan
minnows past: *the coin lost in the river*
is found in the river. I sink and rise
between gravities—not silt or pebble,
crawdad or tadpole, downstream or up—
but the sun's currency, fired and wanton,
the moon's hoarded bullion, the pearl
of impermanence ashore in the muck.

Learning to Glide

Yesterday's Subaru a brute in comparison,
    the wind has its way with her,
        buffeted by October, the leaves jazzed

as kites. I'm along for the ride, the new
    hybrid teaching me to lift my lead foot,
        anticipate the slope, the light changing

three blocks down, to remember that time
    really is on my side, no destination but
        the journey, never mind the fuel economy,

prideful MPG lauded on PriusChat,
    the stealth stop. My wheels hover
        over asphalt, the diamond earth's

sudden springs, sinking sand. Some days
    I quake at the thought of arrival,
        others I pulse in fits and starts,

I glide.

IV

If you look, the lost and found will glitter all their lessons.

—Susan O'Dell Underwood, "Empathy"

Inner Work

for Paula Capps Kyser

The inner work must be done in the well
of drawer among pebbled buttons kept

for whenever, lavender sachets spilling
their guts, Grandmama's cat's-eye glasses,

my pride pierced on her pincushion.
Only there can I sift what hangs loose

on my shoulders, the stained, the torn,
crocheted illusories never seeing

light of day. Keys to nowhere, Irish
pence, the pocket Psalms and Proverbs

have no providence, no commerce
in my wilderness, though I rub each

faux pearl as talisman, the Long Nights Moon
heartsick at my window. Strayed, undone

in the layers, I dig to the bottom, wooden
thud that nips my heel, turns me to the field

of what never emptied in the first place,
not bargain or plea but steppingstones,

uneaten breadcrumbs, one then another.
Buckeye and amethyst still harbor luck.

Old stockings will do for garden stakes,
for spring coming sure.

Figs in Old October

> All things on earth point home in old October.
> —Thomas Wolfe

Those let go too long drip on late roses,
ant fogged, overfull of September—no kin
to the last beefsteaks embittered on the vine.
Day by day they turn, verde to gold, under
high-hatted leaves, my cupped hand the opposite
of drought and waiting. The youngest won't ripen
before first frost—over sixty seasons tell me
as I cradle this bearing. Call it aureole or labia,
the body's sweet held and bartered in old October,
when all things compass home—loves spent
in regret, gone to earthly hollow, loves milky
at the stem taken whole for the teeth. October,
when late musk enters my fruited dreams,
    hung in winter's false light.

The Out Breath Longer Than the In

Take in the acorns
popping underfoot, the sheepdog's nose
at hinge of knee, take in the plentiful mast
forecast this winter for the Smokies, that part
of the breath ragged and blue from snowfall
closing 441, piggybacked on September drought,
the spell for rain useless as wedding gardenias
in leathered cellophane.

Take it in, neither
drawing up my height nor bellowing
my chest, but curled under ribs like sage
lit at the lintel, uncertain if I'm coming
or going, the ash of failed days still sweet
and blacking my thumbs.

Now the out breath,
children slapping feet on pavement,
flip-flops on hot tar, summer melons
cut with salt, with mint, with honey.
The bright world winnows to an end
I somehow knew would arrive
in gray dawn.

Leave a stray refrain,
my father's last bed and hours, rubbed coin
of spent marriage. Give it out like alms
to the homeless, tin cup with some rattle left,
some crooked music when the crank is turned
and the monkey clinks cymbals then slows
to dying. Give it up and out, the breath
no longer yours or mine, not caught
or held or sung but flown.

Pie Lee

Through the bed railing, our game
to pass time in the ER: he pokes out
a hand, we shake, he draws back,

laughing. Nearly midnight in the ER,
again my father slips to the fence
of his old backyard, reaches

to the little neighbor girl who peels
foil from Juicy Fruit. So young,
she is unable to say his full name:

Phillip Lee. She pokes gum
through the wire, draws back, laughing:
Pie Lee, Pie Lee, you can't catch me.

Unable to say his name, my father
criss-crosses the wiring in his brain,
its young lights long past midnight's

hour. So long our wait, he draws
back the rumpled bedsheet, floor
blue cold beneath his feet.

Our game pokes time through
uncertain gain, little child I tend
this night rails against those lesser

lights. All the girls he might catch
just past his reach, growing so
like tendered fruit the other side
                of the fence.

Intervention

I was wearing it most days,
braided horsehair bracelet from Cody,
our second Wyoming trip—or it was wearing
me, umbilicus of undoing, frayed history
on my sleeve, my unletting go like July snow
on the path to Jenny Lake, the lupined Tetons
hushing our breath. Even then, our long
mane uncoiled end to end. I know
where it fell that day

in the parking garage
my purse slumped to my wrist, someone
came along, bent to its delicate plaits,
what luck, and slipped it on, just like that,
the day fate released our little circle,
remnant of the Old West, noose cut
at the moment of truth—to keep risking
that cautionary salt or walk on.

Near Drowning

Out past the whitecaps something not bird
or buoy, something struggling—and we stop
walking as the sky pinks like the inner lip
of mussels, as others have stopped to clump
and point, and the owner comes along saying
his dog swims out all the time, *no problemo*,
but this time the riptide's strong below the hook
of Pawleys and no one's happy with the owner,
who launches his kayak, soon turning tail
in the high surf, outpaced by a motorized kayak,
a stranger slicing the waves for the sake
of this exhausted marvelous dog that has captured
every heart, especially my oldest granddaughter,
terrified in the thrall of rescue, though it all
works out—the stranger grabs his scruff,
the sheriff zooms in and ski-doos him home,
the owner looks peevish and sheepish
and not loved by anyone.

Drowning's always near, lashed to our mast
of overconfidence, like the year the youngest
girl walked into the pool without her swimmies,
without anyone imagining disaster, except
my daughter, who leapt from the chaise
to seize her child, sputtering minnow,
from the turquoise bottom—that moment
she snatched life from the splash of distraction,
the older kids knowing to dog paddle
in the deep end, noon bearing down,
the parents blind to every other possibility,
thinking *out there*, far out in the surf, spins
the real danger, though it all worked out—
little fish flopped on dry land, all of us gasping
for good air, so harrowing we rarely repeat it,

as if retelling would burst some dream
that still imagines the miraculous.

Busy in the bardo of dailiness, I bent
from one horizon to another, leaping
over crushed shells. I sometimes forgot
to breathe the air right in front of me,
so ordinary I rarely spoke of it—I forgot
the raucous summers in Calabash
that burned my most delicate parts,
even as they healed tight and glossy.
I forgot how quickly distraction rolls in
from the east, how sand shifts underfoot.
I thought the riptide, spinning far out, past
the barrier islands, wasn't meant for me—
a competent swimmer, after all. Like any evening
at the Carolina beach when Vereen's men
cast their seines for spots, when the horizon
bows to the sea and the sky's fine pink
is a mussel shell, I thought the walk
to the pier so safe. In the split second
between terror and grace, I never imagined
the eye of grief's vortex, rusted hook
of a marriage ending.

Animal Spirits

for Eleanor and Vivian

Even as cubs, my granddaughters
guard me, though they know no grief
or brokenness, no empty house jangling,
tap at death's gate. They preen their pelts,
crouch on ready haunches in halogen glare—
the unstoppable traffic, intentional swerve,
sweet dish of poison. They prowl for me,
howl with me in the spilt strawberry moon,
raw-hearted tributes left on my stoop.
I shall fear no evil, their shadows large ahead,
behind. I shall not falter in age or decline,
for the path they prepare is clothed in light.

Hear them answer blood's love call,
snag in their teeth the arrowed night.

Frankie Bear

No need, no want, not me, not mine,
silent chant as I sit zazen, my cushion

purple for mystery, for magic. All well
and good until his tongue on my hand.

He would keep me here, sprawl belly up
in the nest my legs make, until light

unshutters my drift to transcendence,
until time has no tune or meaning.

He would loll as he does while I'm away
each day—gone his polestar, his lamb

to steer homeward—fur shed like fleece
on fencewire, on the futon, the club chairs,

green and rose, trying this one and that
before I return from the deep forest,

a gathering of quince and hazelnuts.
This tufted trail I follow with more need

and want than I admit in my practice
of *not me, not mine.* Runes followed,

moon or no, into what magic makes
of morning, what mystery makes

    of my untried life,
    licked and licked awake.

Wayfinder

Wandering the maze of hospital corridors
to see a new doctor, I'm past pregnant
trimesters and hoped-for heartbeat,
that blessed *whoosh-whoosh*, past even
the iron-red tide. I know what's ahead:
chill speculum, snap of latex glove,
heels tense in the stirrups. At the information
desk I see my neighbor, bright and ready
to herd me, lost sheep, to Building A,
not B. The elevator opens as she says,
I'm a wayfinder. My job is to take you
where you need to be.

A doctor's muffled confessional
bleeds through the wall as I wait,
the anointing of family oil: depression,
alcoholism, cardiovascular event,
colon and breast cancer, melanoma.
History coming as it comes—untreatable,
snowblind, hooded for the last clean shot.
I wait, am waiting still, for the downrush
of storied wings, folded or outspread,
for the wayfinder whose job is to lead me
back to whatever blessing is possible,
through the *whoosh* of doors
that, despite my errancy, open.

At My Father's Hospital Bedside

> He rode with the sun coppering his face
> and the red wind blowing out of the west.
> —Cormac McCarthy, *All the Pretty Horses*

We've come from the upcountry down to this mess,
as my father says, without a penny, scared to death.
In deepening haze, tubes looping his wrists burn
collapsed veins, drip the bloodied sun. Cinched
and hobbled, he's stronger than we both realize—
greenbroke roan driven from the chalk mesa
trembling to first see man afoot. I press my head
to his chest to talk the terror out, run my daughter's
veil along his muzzle. I say no harm will come
in this iron twilight, scratch his name in the golden
dust so quickly flown. *Phillip, lover of horses.*
The near firmament pitches and rears as I whisper
a picturebook of the open plains: *yo y yo solo,*
as I slip on the dark reins.

Into the Water

> The water is wide, I cannot get o'er /
> Neither have I the wings to fly.
> —Scottish ballad

He's so small, the moment I pass the second-
story window. A man at the mouth of the creek
walks further in, the water widens, deepens

into more than creek. He parts the flow
like a razor, where he's headed no one
can stop him. Maybe down to Meridian

or Gulfport in that late '60s Bonneville,
hawking Toro tillers and mowers slick
as owlshit with his Alan Ladd looks.

My feet nailed to the floor, as so often
in dreams, my voice cotton dry. The current
cursive at the knees, his pants, the hard crease

he insists on, dark and leaden. A river now,
brown as his Maduros, rising to his chest,
still he walks, beyond terror or calling out

to someone with the power to save or redeem,
beyond the pale of nightmare, so that when
I rush in and pull him to the dream shore,

kneel on thick dream mud, shake my father
from dreamed unrest, only I awaken, only
I am swimming madly to the possible light.

Be Peace

Stone for my pillow, no cover
for my bed, another night wrestling

Jacob's angels for a rung up the ladder—
visitation of dead dog, dead love moldering

in the garden's back corner. Not even
ring-eyed sleeplessness calms my dragon

nature. I exhale heat and havoc, mishmash
of what happened on its endless reel.

Venus in retrograde, Mercury in Leo,
misalignments and stirrings, the forever gone.

The eight worldly winds of samsara swirl—
wheels grind out sorrow, blame, retribution.

In the green chair, I picture the rowboat's
sway, petals of jade light, the riverrock's

descent into quiet. I sink in over my head.
Two herons trace an awkward contrail,

nothing like kitetails or bridal veils,
but signs of lives cast off, flown far.

Impossible blessings I breathe in,
pure as burned sage—the breath

      unswayed, rooted in everything
      sacred and still, even peace.

Dogma

His stare a laser
through my closed eyes, he doesn't
care I've left the awareness of my body
in half-lotus on a borrowed cushion.
He doesn't care when I'm in cat position
on the rug, easing kinks, hoarded grief
in joint and tendon, working to be less
and less. Paws on my legs break the fourth
wall of intention. He nudges in, whether
I'm about to unearth the world's oyster
at the bottom of pooled questions, whether
its luster is for me alone, opening me
to wonder, or just sinking further
into loss, cool mud and silt, the aching
bliss of it all.

No Grief

> You have to sit in the very bonfire of distress,
> and you sit there until you're burnt away.
> And it's ashes, and it's gone.
> —Leonard Cohen

The world bends to no one's weep
and wail, except maybe the rose-tipped
grasses in early fall, the garden that's mine

to neglect in long drought, which I did,
parched with change, the brick of grief
in my pocket now airy as a whistle.

Except maybe the dreams searching,
searching for the one who left, though
now the house, hearth to counter, hums

along with the whistle. Caring how
the world bends or doesn't is the opposite
of my gleaning in light's descent

in the pasture of no grief no self no past,
except that it bends, I know it does, the world
willow not oak, on impermanent winds.

Except that bonfires under my breastbone
bear me across the banks of weep and wail,
the lilt of my soles on hot coals,

my body burnt through, unbent.

After the Final Decree

          This morning
I awaken with no power, but no,
power is with me blood and breath,
earthed on oak floor, garden soil—
persicaria's Red Dragon, the bee-loud
buddleia. So this morning I awaken
with no electricity, but no, my surge
completes a circuit crown to heel,
the ions and anions
my unreckoned force.

          I could say
I woke with no lights, but not
that either, for I bend to life's cruelties
knowing they fish the same stream
as the sharer of his catch, for my heart
empties of leaden samsara, refills
with mother's milk. Truer, the morning
begins in yesterday's faithless
blue dark, mere spark
of my possible voltage.

With Me

With me as I build in the home of myself,
careful to wet the bricks else my joints
buckle, walls tumble of impatience. With me
as I smudge the house of ghosts, of circumstance

and happenstance, the bitter end's swear
now blown milkweed. With me picking figs,
leaves speaking salt and rough going,
my reach for the highest up, deepest in,

hidden under. With my bones of contention,
the red middle, gristle crossways in my throat,
all the failed heart knows in one swallow.
With my liminal ache, time of day the French

call *entre chien et loup*, between dog
and wolf, world and otherworld, my dusk
not yet blue-black or brimming twilight.
With my father's descent to the field

sunken with the sum of his travels,
my own bag of bones packed for farewelling,
when the muscled catastrophe has its day,
charnel ground littered with and without

my say-so, the false idols fallen
to paste, the last ecstasy passed
into blessing, into hard surrender.